IN HER I AM

IN HER I AM

CHRYSTOS

PRESS GANG PUBLISHERS

Some of the poems in this collection have been previously published
in Chrystos' books *Not Vanishing* (1988) and *Dream On* (1991), also
available from Press Gang Publishers. "Song for a Lakota Woman" was
originally published in *Lesbian Culture: An Anthology,* eds. Julia Penelope
and Susan Wolfe (Freedom CA: The Crossing Press, 1993).

CANADIAN CATALOGUING IN PUBLICATION DATA
Chrystos, 1946 –
In her I am
Poems.
ISBN 0-88974-033-X
1. Lesbians – Poetry. 2. Lesbianism – Poetry
I. Title.
PS3553.H5715 1993   811'.54   C93-091795-2

First Printing September 1993
94 95 96 97 98   6   5   4   3   2

Edited for the press by Barbara Kuhne
Front and back cover photographs by Chick Rice
Design and typesetting by Valerie Speidel
Typeset in Adobe Caslon
Printed on acid-free paper by Kromar Printing Limited
Printed and bound in Canada

Press Gang Publishers
101 - 225 East 17th Avenue
Vancouver, B.C.
Canada v5v 1A6

This book is in memory of Sapphocat
my deer companion of 19 years
(my longest relationship)
who enjoyed watching sex from the corner of my bed
often purring so loudly
that my lovers & I laughed,
and for the poet Sappho, her namesake
whose fragments of Lesbian Erotica
we cherish
as the oldest surviving record
of our natural existence

When I came out in 1965 at 19, into the working-class bar world of San Francisco (does anyone remember Romeo's on Haight Street?), the butches wore leather jackets, dildoes were common & I wore high heels when I dressed to go out, as well as far too much sticky make-up   The rejection of this very sexual culture by feminist Lesbians has marred my relationship with Women's Liberation from the beginning   My life rarely exists in Lesbian texts − a current exception is the excellent book *Stone Butch Blues* (by Leslie Feinberg), which often had me in tears

Women's Liberation, the Red Road & the peace movement have all profoundly affected my life, but when I consider what has shaped me most thoroughly, it is my love of Lesbians   I have watched fads come & go, but have always been proud to love Lesbians, even when I was being beat up at the Doggie Diner on Market Street for doing so

I live on a razor: I am only intermittently cherished by the mainstream Lesbian gang, who are primarily caucasian (& not interested in my burning concern for First Nations' struggles), while in Native communities homophobia is inevitable because of the influence of the christian churches   The only time all of my identities come home is during the yearly Gathering we have for Indigenous Lesbians, Gays and our lovers & friends   I live from year to year on those five-day celebrations   (I will comment that Indian Country is becoming less homophobic faster than Lesbianism is coming to understand, rather than appropriate, Native spirituality and culture)

I now live alone on the island I've married, passionately involved with my gardens, writing & art, & with several lovers   It has taken me many years of failed relationships, bitterness & recriminations to understand my sexuality and to be honest with my lovers   I pray that all Lesbians find an honest understanding & enjoyment of their sexuality

Contents

IN HER I AM

You Ask Me for a Love Name

I name you moon bird   diamond frost   night fruit
tender flag   bramble nest   vision bread   proud eye
I call you flying your tongue lifts me radiant
fills lost places
I swallow you staining my mouth sweet
with your blackberry nipples
I raise you over my house proclaim you
Clasp your head burrowing between my legs
I paint you watch you like mountains at dusk
Let you
whenever you want with a rush of blue violet spring
I name you darkness which heals
moving over my weariness in stars
I guard you
face you
polish you
Name you pirate with kidnapping grin
I name you fire & fine
I name you this glistening brilliant plumage
I put on my wings
crowing

for Pat

Desire a Blue Fog

in my arms coming through these tall trees of your land
your gift of time
My hands suck your breasts   our mouths know
my eyebrows singe curling
Your belly my horizon
sea where I catch myself glowing teal
Your pink nipples near my dark brown ones tell the roads
& differences between us   Times we've opened
our eyes together every morning
Deaths we've survived
Tears & laughter in my fingers which enter you always new
singing with memories of your wet rose rolling
the wet edge of my tongue a harvest moon of fat gold
Your green leaf eyes part the blue smoke of need
I feel your heart pounding in your rose
cantilevered over the cliff of pines rising
Thousands of kisses our tongues hold each one
I rise to meet your light   a leaf flames under water
haloing the silken web of your fingers
Beating in my throat a blue cry to have you   possess you
to be torn open by your sobbing pleasure
to ride you through silver fog
reaching for thousands of miles
rushing with speed of light to screams again & again
your muscles take me delirious inside of you
my whole body pulsing with your need   Gasping
nothing is left of us but a silver mist we swirl through
flaming the trees with a stillness that moans
our bodies heaving with rich heat

shimmer of water on roads illusory as song
I warm myself with our sounds the anchor of your tongue
that goes so deep
streaming with your juices
I roll pounding
with the blue spirit of you coiling my heart
into a gold rose

Your Fingers Are Still

inside me pulsing
as I vacuum   look at books   wash dishes   cook
ride down the road   open my mail   burn the trash
Your fingers buckle
my knees   Stomach turns over   small moans
escape my lips at the laundromat   grocery store
Your tongue shivering me while I call a new job
pull the covers up on my bed   go to the bank
Smack of your comforting belly as you come on me
as I catch a ferry   iron a shirt   pull weeds
Your fingers don't stop
moving me

I Bought a New Red

dress to knock her socks off, spent all day looking for just the right combination of sleeve & drape, so I could actually knock all her clothes off   She met me at the boat dressed so sharp she cut all the boys to ribbons

Over dinner in a very crowded queer restaurant I teased her by having to catch drips of my food with my tongue, staring into her eyes, daring her to lean over & grab my breast or crotch & titillate the faggot waiters   She sat back soaking me up, enjoying my teasing tidbits, for all the world not wanting to fuck me ever   I knew better as she's kept me on my back all night since we met   I began to pout because I wasn't affecting her enough to suit me & she hadn't said a thing about my dress   Just then the waiter brought our dessert, a small cake she'd had decorated to say *Beg Me To Fuck You,* with pink roses all around the edge

I laughed so hard I tore my dress a little   The waiter smirked   I fed her roses from the cake, she licked my fingers so slowly I almost screamed   Near us some blazer dykes were very nervous & offended, so naturally she began to make loud sucking noises   Laughing, we left them to their girl scout sex & went dancing, where she kept her hand on my ass & her thigh between my legs even during the fast ones   Going home she pulled my thigh-top stockings to my knees & played with me   I'd worn no underpants especially for her   We were having such a good time she couldn't park & we laughed as she tried a third time & I blew in her ear almost causing a wreck

Then we started doing it in the front seat of her car, awkward with gear knob & wrong angles, until a cop pulled up & said sarcastically through the open window *Do you need some assistance parking, Sir?* She flamed as red as my dress & returned to maneuvering the car instead of me

I was so horny I could barely walk in my matching high heels & she held my arm as we crossed to her place, pinching my nipple with her other hand & smiling her grin of anticipation   We necked on the porch to upset her nosy neighbors, who have twice complained about the noise I made coming   Then she couldn't get the lock to work & we giggled as I stood with heels in hand, my stockings full of runs & a wet spot on the back of my silk dress almost as wide as my ass   The door popped open so suddenly she fell forward & I tumbled after her, gasping   I started up the stairs heading for her bed when she caught hold of my pubic hair with her hand & pulled me back onto her until I was kneeling on the stairs as she fucked me from behind & my dress ripped some more as she took me hard, kicking the door shut with her foot, taking me out of this world until I was upside down with my head at the door & leg on the banister   Heat of her crotch as she came on me, my dress ripping right up the front as we laughed harder

The next morning her roommate said we were disgusting & we grinned with pride   The cleaners cannot repair the sweet dress & looked at me very oddly but I went out giggling & made her a pocket handkerchief with it, sewing

rolled hems & a discreet message along one edge   *PLEASE*
rip my dress off anytime

Like a Wing

your tongue brushes me
softly painting
my feathers smooth

We Pretended She Was a Young Boy

who had come over to mow my lawn & I'd asked her in
for a cool drink of lemonade
wearing only a negligee of pink peach silk
& a string of pearls
I made her sit beside me on the couch while I told her
how much I liked her hard body & the fine dew of sweat
on her upper lip
& didn't allow her to touch me
I asked if she needed a little back rub after
working
so hard
because I understood what the sun could do to her
body   Heat clenching in the thighs
I said maybe I could help her relax
I laid her down on the couch & straddled her
the smell of me rising up wetting her jeans
I began to rub her hard
wiggling in just the right way to make her groan
but not letting her touch me
She had the dildo on   rubbing her crotch
as I rocked back & forth whispering softly that I hoped
she felt a little better
until she turned over in a sudden movement & opening
her 501's gave it to me hard
while I pretended to be shocked in delicious protests
my nipples so hard pushing out the silk of our need
She touched me without my permission pulling
the pearls until I touched her lips kissing me hard
her thrusts into me her hands on my hips

the lemonade flying across the room
as I bit her neck coming
so hard

for B.J.

Jump Back In Me Now

She tender whiskers dip me in molasses sucking deep
her back I dreamt in afternoon light
comes to me in rainy 3 A.M.
fingers delicate as rainbows in puddles my ass arcs
she takes me then again
lights fading in the dawn our lips cling
swollen when I wake she's left for work
my nipples reach
to where she lay
burying my face in her smell rolling over laughing
when someone asks me how
I feel
I grin Oh
so good still swollen wet my my my
I'm Natalie's puddle

Against

your skin red under my hand against every
political principle we both hold you want
me to spank you & I do
We're survivors of childhood violence with black eyes
in common from mothers who hated our difference
Neither loves our love
they'd beat it out of us if they could
Your people as well as mine slaughtered in millions
Queer we're still open season
My fingermarks on your ass are loving you
tied to the bed my other hand pushing
into our vortex of pleasure   I'd agree that it's wrong
to do this
Out of our bruised lives should come some other way
This forbidden hand this deep memory this connection
for which I've no explanation against a wall of right
that would define us as victim/aggressor
I want to give you
what you want
although my kind would beat it out of me with words
if they could
My hands guess this is a difference that is a crime
to admit in our small queer world
Desire red & raw as wounds we disguise
we're open season

Hot My Hair Smells of Your Cunt

sheets a hurricane at my throat your kisses
music   breasts pressing into my back   my ass
in the air wanting it
Your hands moonlight on water enter me
blazing my mouth swollen
tongue thick between your thighs
echoes I carry of our nights which light my fingers
remembering how wet you blossom your muscles
balloon out return rippling tides   my heart
catches spinning silver our lips one quivering moon
reflected

Dare

She sighs away from me, turning in pale sheets damp with our night's desire, her brown arms languid, her lips parted, as I listen to the sheer call of crows at dawn   I watch her while she cannot be guarded, ready with witty barbs as she brushes her hair, humming behind the closed doors of her black eyes   Wrens begin singing nearby   Her eyes open like wings stretching   The intensity of my look has awakened her & she turns from me restlessly   She hasn't decided yet whether my need is a burden or a back rest

Kiss me!   I obey, her lips hungry & lazy   *Did you make coffee?*   I shake my hair, no   She is graceful as she rises, pulling her long, large, sensual body into the sky, going to her prayers   This is one of the canyons between us, her traditions of a lifeline, grandmothers, ceremonies tended She looks over at my back door banging in the wind, where I pray without a language, sitting on the steps, watching leaves move   I don't belong in her ceremonies; she thinks I do   Stubborn, I cling to the prayers I made up myself as a child of tenements, alone with drugs, violence, boozy wind of neglect   She longs for my words as I long for her grace, her exactly measured tobacco ties   In this hard desert we are each other's spring cacti blasted into bloom, our eyes darting to rocks which might be more reliable than either of us

When she flirts with others, I bury my irritation in recognition of my identical play with dirty words, suggestive glances, hints of thirst   There will always be women who want her   She'll respond if she's in the mood

When I watched her cross a field, so long ago, at the first
Gathering, her skirt shimmered in the heat, her laughter
was a flower   I knew loving her would terrorize me with
the demons of jealousy   I watch them as I have watched
other demons, until acceptance is possible   One could not
call it peace

She teases me about the first night we lay together, her
nakedness inflaming the bed as I cowered in sweatpants, my
hands rammed into pockets   I did not sleep all night, eras-
ing in a futile loop the burning sweat of denied passion
She laughs, telling strangers that the so-called sex maniac
didn't even touch her   In my defense, I had her stories in
my throat where they lay numb   Of her other lover, whose
violence had hospitalized her, that lover still screaming after
her, that lover she was escaping as she lay with me, that
lover to whom she would return after our brief 4 days, that
lover she would take more than 2 years to rip away from,
that lover whose eyes terrified me when I met them later
She gave me the story of her incest, the story of her confu-
sion   I cannot take a woman who does not specifically, cer-
tainly, without shame, without hesitancy, want me   I can't
be an escape route anymore, my back hurts too much

She asks me to build her a white picket fence, a home, a
forever, to love her & no other   I despise fences & climbed
over them as soon as I could walk   Fences are psychosis,

unreal   I know that she wants me to build the fence so she can jump over it, to watch what I'll do   Her monogamy is as seasonal & quixotic as my own   She lies as beautifully too

I want us to live in a wide place, where all our canyons & arroyos are known, respected   I want to live with her in a spring wash of desire   I want our wanderings to cross & recross each other with a wind blowing away our tracks   I dream of building her a miniature house of cacti with a fence of glass, so slippery & clear that it disappears when she doesn't want it   I paint flowers & make them a box, sending her a fence in a dream   Tie it down with light-ning, thunder, her laughter & skirts brushing the sage   We make a home for each other in our hands, two women whose names appear briefly in the wind of time

In Her I Am

fine dark pulsing without time where I'm meant to be
Clear well fed no words calculating next move
No misunderstanding this muscle which breathes with
my hand
enfolded hot as air vibrating in summer
Slurping my tongue is a cat   feather   river   vortex
an angel   night jasmine   wind licking us clean
We're hurtling through stars becoming
here
as we so rarely are
Heavy with longing to stir ourselves
from ember to embrace
Moaning with you so deeply in you I'm no more than air
to meet your need
Sobbing rocks fly through my heart in a river that breaks
down into my eyes where closed & black I am suddenly
red & searing hot rubies

O Honeysuckle Woman

won't you lay with me
our tongues flowering
open-throated
golden pollen
We could drink one another
sticky sweet & deep
our bodies tracing silver snail trails
Our white teeth nibbling
We could swallow desire whole
fingers caught in our sweet smell
We'd transform the air
O honey woman
won't you suckle me
Suckling
won't you let me
honey you

for Nanci

Top Sadist in Town

We met after a reading by one of my friends, who was staying with Her, but finds Her too dangerous to play with One of the other diners was a very egocentric writer, more so than most of us, one who thinks she must glitter with wit & that peculiar artsy charm, eating up all the air   Bored, I ignored Miss Writer to begin flirting with Her, across the table, intrigued by Her even-more-butch-than-usual style, Her breasts bound, which I hadn't seen since I helped my lover do it in the sixties   I noticed Her eyes were a wall, rigidly maintained   Decided I wanted to know what She was hiding   We agreed to a dinner date   I began plotting what I would wear   As She was leaving I saw a tortured lonely angry child glance out at me for a few moments before Her eyes went flat again   I didn't change my expression, deliberately, so She would assume I hadn't seen   I fell in love

I went out of town on readings, so our dinner date was postponed several times   I invited Her son to come along & offered to have it be my treat   She was intrigued   I brought Her an enormous, awkward bouquet from my garden, which She accepted with uncomfortable grace   I was indulging myself in my old games of turning the bed around on stone butches   At dinner we spoke of books, writing, sex, each of us assessing the other   My friends had warned me about Her, sometimes rather hysterically   She had raped women, She had broken Her ex-lover's eardrum, She was out of control, bad, evil, She would hurt me, why was I being so crazy   Her friends had in turn warned Her that I was vanilla, would say terrible things about Her, hate Her   We had a good laugh at their expense & then I saw where the real danger lay   I wasn't afraid of Her at all & that frightened Her   I've worked the streets, I've escaped men who meant to murder me, my instincts & will to fight as dirty as necessary are still honed in my back pocket, ready, though I live a seemingly more serene life now

As I walked down the street, a little ahead of Her for Her benefit, in my silver backless heels, She admired my legs I'm used to that & use it   One day a butch will admire my mind & I'll notice her in the sea of hands & tongues When we returned to Her home, which was very conventional except for the artfully arranged whips, leather masks & handcuffs, I admired Her curtains & was pleased that She had made them Herself, a rich medieval swirl of flowers patterning the room as stained glass would have   I mused on the connections between s/m & the churches, the priest I used to whip on Fridays at noon in the old Jack Tarr Hotel   One of my steadiest customers   I often wondered if he paid me from the poor box that had fed me as a child

I examined Her bookcase & was not impressed, though She meant me to be   She had been an intellectual about 10 years ago, from the gist of the titles   There were no significant feminist works & almost nothing by People of Color I realized that She hated women passionately, hated being a woman, wanted to kill my vulnerability, sharp reminder of Her own in some faded memory, not knowing that I wear my vulnerability as a mask to protect the steel underpinnings of my heart   I've seen variations of this hatred in other lovers' eyes

She showed me the whips She'd made, which were beautifully crafted   I described the dress I want, of red leather with boning for my large breasts, open about four inches wide all down my back & laced with black silk   She offered to make it   I knew She was only seducing me   She was surprised that Her whips didn't frighten me, the echo of Her friends' warning voices   Whips neither scare me nor appall me   They're simple symbols of oppression, with no erotic charge   I could feel that She was intrigued by my boredom, interpreting it to mean that perhaps I was even more kinky than She   I am   She read me a gory sex story that She had written   I've read all of the marquis de sade & I unfairly compared it   As I remember, Her sadist tortured someone to death & then either fucked the dead body or ate the remains   I was reminded of teenage boys & grade B horror movies, the kind where the props are too obviously props

I was bored, thinking She wouldn't be any fun at all to fuck because She was more interested in the stage set than my body   Decided I'd just go home & have a good time with my own dildo   She became hyper-alert, a hunter about to lose the spoor   She told me She could see that I'd given up the idea of sleeping with Her so now She wanted to She likes to rearrange the furniture in women's heads, She said   I'm far more interested in rearranging the contents of my own head, especially in words   Controlling others is as uninteresting as whips   It's far too common a preoccupation   I shrugged & thought, well, I can rearrange again later when She's done thinking She possesses me   No one ever has   When I'm done I walk out

As we came near Her bedroom door, She announced that all who entered there must ask permission   I laughed a rich spontaneous belly laugh, sure She was joking, & sashayed right through   Later my friend said that I had violated Her boundaries & been very rude   I laughed then too   Either you want to fuck me or you don't, games are for children

Her room was painted a green that echoed the nuthouse, which made me laugh again   She probably thought I was nervous but I was amused by Her inferior decoration   I've worked for so many rich people that I've become a snob by osmosis   The bed was set at a dramatic angle from the wall, with black polyester satin sheets & a large sword pointing down at the head   Black candles, of course   A perfect place to stage a lesbian version of "Medea"   Various tools of Her trade were laying around but we'd agreed to have so-called vanilla sex, so they were lifeless witnesses to a long night

As She was not really interested in the art of making love, our foreplay was wooden   She did not undress, keeping

Her black T-shirt as a barrier, tough   She was packing, which I had enjoyed all through dinner, restraining myself from stroking Her sweet bulge only because of Her son

I raised my legs & our plumbing lesson began   I veered from arousal to thinking of a piece I'd been working on that afternoon, words always more compelling than reality, or perhaps the only way I can stand reality: my own black T-shirt   We ground on, She had several orgasms, I came close a few times but my body was wiser than myself & refused to give Her anything

I thought of the man who raped me as a child for so long, his eyes were green too, though this was not rape, it was worse, as we were both absent   I remembered all the boys in high school who had fucked me in exactly the same disinterested way, because it was expected, it proved something, not because they liked sex or me   I saw Her stark cold lonely child again, quickly covered   I imagined that we could do this a few more times & maybe my body would remember how to come without emotion or connection, in that dangerous land of dominance he called love   I wondered as She fucked me if She was bored, because I knew it was a mercy fuck – pain & control are Her blueberry hill   After an hour or so I wanted to be on top   She said She didn't let anyone on top, ever   I pushed Her, purred that it wouldn't kill Her to let me sit on Her dick as it's easier for me to come that way   I loved riding Her, my breasts slapping

In the morning She was sweet but in a hurry & tired, late for work   I noticed how conventional She looked in Her uniform   Recognized Her fascination with s/m − it's the only place She's found to be unique   Writing is my place & perhaps I'm a sadist myself, wanting final control of reality, to carve words with my own knife, leaving scars other lovers have protested in vain

Her son stayed home from school with a sore throat, so I went to the store to buy him juice & left then to go to my own job, with a blister on my baby toe from those new shoes & no other mark on my body, despite the warnings of my pals

She didn't call again   I haven't seen Her in over a year   I resisted the urge to send Her red roses when the night of May 14 returned   I've guessed She probably doesn't even remember me   Am surprised by the depth of my hurt, because I was sure I'd shielded myself to be used without consequences

Love opened despite my anger, despite unsatisfying sex I wouldn't repeat, despite Her   I wondered if it was exactly *to* spite Her, as She'd warned me not to fall in love with Her   I said that if I did, I'd never tell Her   Lies are one of my tools   I craft them carefully, beautifully, with hooves of animals   As time has passed I've silently congratulated Her for hurting me in the deepest place, for winning   I've stopped sending Her witty, provocative postcards from various readings, needling Her until She moved   I've stared at this self-destructiveness of which She is only a faint trace   I've rearranged these words until I've seen what should have been clear to me: She'll never call me because I'm not frightened of Her, could not even pretend for Her sake to be frightened, would never obey Her, have not given my true power to anyone & this frightens Her more deeply than I can imagine   Scratch the bully & find a coward   I'm newly aware of how dangerous I am in the furniture-moving department

She joked about liking to fuck bimbos & I teased Her on one of my postcards about Her bimbo parade, smug in the knowledge that I'm not a bimbo, which is also, I reflect, why She hasn't called   I lied when I let Her believe She had control

She revealed much about my relationships up to that point, a sharp lesson in why they often became so abusive   I seem to be someone easy to shove around, & I am   But I return to where I intended to go in the first place, a trick I learned in order to survive my mother & father & uncle   Let them seem to control you so that you can do what you want   I understand how infuriating I've been, hiding behind a wall of passivity, convinced I was a victim   Rigid   I love Her for what I've seen in myself as a result of Her silence   I love the child She hates & conceals   I don't want to see her again either   I'm afraid of how much I've changed

I catch a sharp whiff of my armpit, which tells me I'm afraid as I write this   Afraid of the censure of those who would say I'm sick to love Her even though there is no relationship between us   Who don't want me to explore what s/m means or to hear that writing is dominance & control, which we don't acknowledge   Afraid of those who will be angry that this is not a sexy story or angry because it violates Her privacy, reveals aspects that are unflattering, explores what is meant to remain a mystery to everyone who is not susceptible to its power   Afraid of the disgust of those who do not recognize themselves in Her as I have or who want to insist that one of us is bad   I know that She was as hurt by my lack of fear & by my laughter as I was by Her silence That if She recognizes Herself in these words She will wonder if I am not the greater sadist

Looking back over my shoulder, I see She's frozen in scars I'm leaving   My legs, still beautiful, long & graceful, are moving to new lovers, unafraid & still dangerous

Close Your Eyes

Come
into a deep dark flower   night woman   inside
crescent moon petals   Scratch your back on this magenta
Roll around in scarlet   Wake Up   Open fur lips
eat your saffron supper   Lick her   Tongues in your fingers
taste her midnight bloom with thirsty skin
Hold her petals of teal   lime   russet   silver
white light gold grass on a summer sleeping hill
stroke this blue gray cradle
These petal colors of dreamtime
realtime in her hidden flower   Here!   Listen!   Now melts
Take off your think-about-it clothes
Leave your answers in the closet
Come for her petals glowing   eyes open along your arms
in this place   her secret mouth   her planting smell
We'll wet
these snow petals   pale peach petals
early morning lavender petals
See her in the deep holding time   floating colortime
coming hometime   Climb into her silver melon breast
held in the noplace of petals   Downy
Here's a dance singing
here's a place to gurgle   laugh   sucking
warm sweet   sweet   in her curly midnight flower
Lotus of a thousand skies   Each color an opening
your eyes lick her
sun yellow   moon blue   pine green   sunrise pink
into her night flower   her moon bloom
inside her dark fur corolla

Roll yourself wet
red   salmon   sepia   mud brown   violet   gold
Paint your mouth in petals
Stay

A Soft Indentation

in my body where yours slept around me
like the gold grass hollow
deer leave in the morning meadow
or the curve of a whale rib
beached on the rocks
I carried back to admire
along the path to my door
A tenderness is yours I feel for
the mountain which centers my life
We are wary of old words used
to describe these circles
We awaken at dawn   leave each other dreaming
slip into the wild edge where reason fails
your branches shelter
mine flower

Song for a Lakota Woman

As we came
around the curve
of a bluff   the lake opened on spread wings
of a white egret
You turned to me with tiny wildflowers in your hands
murmuring softly *Winyan Menominee*
Anpetu Kin Lila Wasté
All my feathers shone in your voice
Brushing through leaves growing from fiery earth
we came to a place where we knew
our mouths would meet
Hurrying to an anonymous room
we showered & plunged into bed
Your soft arms shining brown over me turning
me wild in your hands
a flying lake you drank
flowers in your eyes
as I shouted too loudly coming
open

for KM

Translation of Lakota words:
Menominee woman, you are good & beautiful

Sestina

Taking you my fist becomes a rose
opening into our journey where wings
move over deep water dark with my tongue curling
into your screaming joy your flushed red breasts
Trail of crimson petals I paint along your throat
Your thighs clench my head until I'm near the edge

of losing breath flying into this dawning edge
where our hearts pound one drum   Our bed a rose
As I open my eyes drift slow   Your throat
flutters alive dancing hungry with bright wings
My free hand reaches to stroke your breast
My cheeks wet with your dark hair curling

I'm open to your scarlet openness curling
through my veins   Our bodies blurred no edge
to cut our tongues   My heart dark within my breast
Our fingers twine   My lips suckle your nipples rose
Air soft with songs of our flushed wings
as joy moves deeply red in my humming throat

You suck my toes dancing my throat
open   White water heats rushes through my curling
blood   My thighs tremble open   Touch wings
of your tongue as you fling me into this edge
of silken red flowers blurring to rose
I gasp   Squeeze my dancing breasts

My mouth desperate hot to suck your breast
I find you deep growling in the dark your throat
painting inside my skin with roses
My eyes wet petals   My fingers curling
as you lift my ass & enter me edge
to edge so deep I find my hungry wings

soaring out my love clenches & rises wings
behind my back opening in my breast
reaching joy thick & drifting to an edge
of losing walls   All my cries pulsing open-throated
Deep inside my hungry petals curling
around your hand which must be a rose

Our thighs rose   Wildly throbbing our throats
still sing our wet breasts   Our spirits curling
deep within our dancing edges where we are all wings

You Know I Like To Be

bossed around in the sack but honey don't you be tellin me
what to do anywhere else cause you see I need to run my
own time & if I want to talk & talk & talk for 3 hours on
the phone with my best girlfriend you know you'd better
find yourself something else to do   You do what you need
to be doing & I'll do the same   My pussy is yours when I
say you can have some   Otherwise she belongs to me & if
I want to give her a vacation or 2 with some other fine
woman, doesn't mean there's any less for you   You be vaca-
tioning your own self & I won't say a word   Possession is a
drug-related offense & it offends me when anyone wants to
put a dog collar on me, visible or invisible, cause I ain't no
bitch   I'm my own damn woman & I like all kinds of trou-
ble   But no screaming matches, no stuff about how you
can't live without me because you know I ain't your lungs
I intend to redefine those 4-letter words, Miss Love & Miss
Fuck, with my own body   Let's see each other when it's
good & take a break when it's hard   You're not my woman
& I'm not yours except when I'm coming   Doesn't mean I
love your ass any less   Means I love you more than some
2-bit teenage romance, honey means I love you like a good
woman should

for Bo

Woman

will you come with me moving
through rivers to soft lakebeds
Come gathering wild rice with sticks
Will you go with me
down the long waters smoothly shaking
life into our journey
Will you bring this gift with me
We'll ask my brother to dance on it
until the wildness sings

for Leota

This Is

the blackberry jam I picked & boiled in swift sky August
mooning over your arrival in November
I imagined with sweet anticipation licking
the corners of your mouth dark with fruit
smiling as your soft Brooklyn voice
murmurs *You made this?   Really?*
Yes I wandered searching for the fattest ones
their skins gleaming purple
tearing my bare arms as I reached   stooped
my fingers crimson & rose madder
planning to stir you
as I watched the limpid water wash silver to shore
Sun a blur in these blue swallow arrows of desire
I made this jam sure of your pleasure
thinking of your fingers & lips stained with me
I left it tart pungent as this longing
to spread you sweetly over me

Four Hours Later

when you finally
let me come
screaming so loudly
the upstairs neighbors
pound the floor
my body is your leaf
shivering with each wind
of your tongue
Your hand inside me pulls apart sense
I speak in tongues   weep
Across the room you beckon   my belly contracts
Your smile of satisfaction makes my knees Marcybutter
Sheet-burns on your elbows glow red & tender as my need
You want a poem to make all the clits listening
hard
sliding down in their chairs drooling
I want to keep you all to myself
in the best blues sense
All wet
I want you to keep me that way

All the Best Butches

roll over in the dark but sometimes pretend they don't
Like my sweet fist when they've had their way & mine
with me
Swagger enough to catch my eye
but not enough to bore
Flirt behind their girlfriend's back
because they're as greedy as me
Have a permanent pussy glint on their lips
& smile like dark chocolate
They'll suck your fingers at a restaurant
use their toes under the tablecloth
after you pull their boot off
Stand behind you in a smoky bar & lean over
with a husky whisper to say
Are you busy tonight?
All the best butches never make it to work on time
when they fall in love
Call long distance just to hear my voice
know exactly how
to bring out the best in me

Double Phoenix

She speaks burgundy birds
blue gold wings   flowers indolent on her breasts
she moves slowly her hair curled tightly
hands skimming my thighs she whispers into my ear
I want you   my vulva shivers clenches
her mouth takes me her
tongue tells long dancing stories
of flight stars darkness burst
fingers flicker in my bones
she enters me in the moment when my blood begs her
hard deep light lifts from my lips
whirls   moves tightly   her mouth shivers
Birds appear in my hands
My toes skim stars
I'm wings in the night sky crying out in her breasts
my hips wet flowers

for Peggy

Tongue in Cheek of Horse

Hey I thought I saw you riding by on a white horse
but you say you don't believe in that goo
Wonder if you'd still say so if you'd seen
yourself with plumes in your hat down to the ground
naked with starry spurs
a cape of comets & eyes pure silver moons
You wrote constellations with your lips
Your horse moved like a river with wings of petals
so fast I caught only a glittering glance
Next time you ride by I'll be saddled
ready to go
with goo

for Marti

On the Phone

you whisper in a soft
country drawl
I wanna be
your natural pussy hound
Wanna lick the moon
between your thighs
till my tongue is silver full
Give it to me now
I need
you to burn for me
Wanna hear you gasp
That's right honey
give me some
of your sweet stars
Fly for me howling
down to a hungry dog
ass in the air
I wanna take you
till there's nothing
left but satisfied

for Denise

Despacio

Slowly as petals open our eyes meet
dark to dark each flying away
in our various masks   feathers   costumes
ribbons   rattles   bells   words
We've seduced our bodies
rued consequences to return beside this circle of seeds
Watching warily for the next placement of our feet
I dream of my hands caught in your sweet
black sweep of hair
swimming in the river of your laughter
we're naked in hot sun our breasts wet
with a whole afternoon to roll around
I've given you far more than this rocking pleasure
you acknowledge
I've taken much more than I admit
Drinking your joy as though I've come through a desert
I have
You ask for a new flowering as I'm boarding a plane
I've accepted that you might turn me away at any moment
loving you is to swallow change whole
swooping on brilliant wings
to learn a new language of hint   gesture
delicate as this balancing of iridescence
in our tears shed with shy grace
Let me touch more than your silk skin
Let more than my hand enter you
Let your eyes rest on me drinking deeply

This bouquet I send
is a kiss for each flower
despacio   despacio

para Osita

She Left Me a Note

saying *I DID NOT lick your panties*
must have been my dog
who left them lying in the hallway
Uh-huh I said
NO I really didn't lick your panties
I'm still celibate
Uh-huh uh-huh
Now I'm a sweet woman
so I didn't say
Darlin' you'd better wipe that black lint
from the corners of your lips
Don't worry about it
you can lick my panties anytime

Soft

breasts of fire we live on the water my tongue
drinks you   Wind comes through your tender thighs
I am shaken   You moan the sun changes   Smoke whips
through the air burning on the water
You are a woman who holds me
Could become warm sky here
Fish between your legs gasp for air
We share a good meal
Cook pots full on the water one can see far into the wind
The crying sky changes my tongue whips you burning
I am a woman turning you in my arms like air
holding warm smoke delicious   Your need holds
secret wind   My fingers reach for your burning sky
You are the place of sweet water my hands drink
My breasts on your belly   Place where burning becomes
Time fishes for new water moaning
A place where each stroke could be as slow
as breathing smoke   Your belly makes circles of pleasure
on the water   Opening I gasp for life
Clear place where water & fire meet
Moan of wind in my hair
you could touch me & light a fire
My hands hold you a bouquet of lush
flowers on fire   Tall & stately my tongue
takes you down
to the water where we live

So Baby

you asked
Was it my leather jacket made you want me?
Uh-uh, it was those green diamonds in your blue eyes
Your laughter while you sang me country western hits
across the Porthole table at the top of your lungs
Way you held your glass with fine broad fingers
Sweetness of the way you danced with me
hands doing a tango all over my back
How you chuckled about the thick Oklahoma mud
up on my fancy city girl boots
as we walked in the parking lot
not kissing yet
till I could get so I'd
want to too much
So the next time
when you said all you really
wanted
was to kiss me
there was no answer left but yes
& I turned up country right with my toes dancing on air
screaming into a pillow the first sweet night
you sang between my legs

for Denise

I Suck

her toes, bite her arch, trail my tongue along the inside of
her leg & wait   She groans, pushes her hips toward me   I
smile & return to sucking her toes   Take my time with the
back of her knees, small sucking bites while she wiggles
Lift her thighs onto my shoulders, kneading her ass, my
finger greased as I slide along her crack, teasing   Slap her
pussy as she tries to pull me down with her knees   My
tongue aching for her petals but waiting until the moment
when I feel her urgency greater than mine   She pulls my
hair in a fury of need until my lips touch her curly wetness
I kiss her everywhere except where she wants me   Her clit
fat & erect   I bite her hair with my teeth, pulling   What
do you want, Baby?   *You KNOW*   No, I've never done this
before you'll have to tell me what to do   *LICK ME*   I lick
her once from her cunt to her belly & rise to suck her
breasts   She pounds my shoulders, scratching my back
until I suddenly remember how to eat pussy, how much I
love to eat pussy, how I could have pussy before & after
every meal & would definitely snap up a job in the lesbian
whorehouse eating pussy   My tongue is slow looking for
the path down into the lights of need   I am her pleasure,
focused   I'm erased into the fruit of her flowering, colors
spinning   I follow her through fear   through shame
through cold memories into the valley where pleasure shim-
mers in a spring haze

Her voice leaping pushes sound her body bites the air in a
long sobbing scream roaring her head banging the wall her
fists pounding we're an arch of rainbow as I hang on to her

thighs my nose banging her cunt clenching my hand so
tightly it's numb & I feel her let go into that flamingo pink
sea vibrating lavender to magenta

Did you come a little bit, Baby?   *Oh FUCK you*
Oh please do
As soon as you can move

for Marti

Na' Natska

Teasing your eyes flicker like tongues on my lips
little roses your nipples become red mountains
My tongue climbs into you
shaking our legs sweat sliding
Your fingers in me are ruby-throated
humming birds   Your eyes iridescent wings
Deep I open   my stomach rises to meet your hands
wet with me   I suck your fingers
You laugh a gurgle of nectar
We go shining in the rainy road your palm kneading
my thigh   mine yours
I murmur   *Am I affecting your driving too much?*
Tossing your head smiling you answer
I want you to
All day I'm wet as I paint
while you study falling asleep after 26 pages of greek
I roll in you like first snow melt shocking my blood
with this glistening new
river of humming birds between us

for Alice

Fragrant Cloud

You land in my garden as the first rose
blazes open
deep coral as the flames in my fingers
when I touch you

para Osita

Bright In Your Dark Mouth

your tongue sliding along your lips pink
as you lick words
Thoughts drift across your face
You're telling me of the woman you want
fighting to walk off the ruts you've known
I watch your tongue
your eyes where I could glide in
my body a glimmer in their black luster
You're onyx   a molasses woman
tall with muscles on your back   long feet
You dance on coals
You speak of her   I watch you
my lips drifting through a seduction scenario
where I polish your skin until you reflect light
Your pink tongue tending mute places in my body
wants to cradle yours
I sit on my hands to stop from cupping your breasts
as your shirt leans open
We embrace good-bye   good friends
Your mouth still wet with crumbs of her
mine wet
with wanting your pink tongue to speak to me
without words

2 A.M. I'm Licking

my lips because yours are sleeping 2,000 miles away
in the bed you chased me around
spilling water   knocking over candles
pillows cascading to the floor
blankets love-knotted   sheets wet
I'm wiggling my ass which still feels the brand
of your hand when you want me
I'm already in Albuquerque where we'll meet
in 7 days for a 48-hour fire
though my plane won't leave until Friday
We'll have to be quieter & less wild staying
with my friends
but I'll still know we're playing hard
& getting to it

for Denise

Sheet Lightning

between my legs as you give me your hot coffee look
across the table eating fried potatoes I've made
My lips swell throb as I hurry off
to where I'm supposed to go
which is the last thing on my mind
Still liquid with your kisses
which break me into warm cream

for Marti

Hold Me Down

tie me to my bed with silk so I can't get away
since I don't want
to anyway
Pull my skirt over my head
face lost in hot ruffles
Fuck me with your strap on
till my pussy sucks
Screaming to let me free I want you
to hold me there in that sharp gasping
before exploding
Grab my hair & wrap it around your fist
growling
make me come
when I beg you to stop
I'm ready to go
over
Make me

Your Iridescent Aqua

Olmeca tongue enters my mouth
quick as the snake which began the world
I slip my long wild rice need around your flaming dance
deep as entering you up to my wrist
your velvet rose cunt blossoming wide
I lick your ass
as you moan laughing
Baby you're making me
wet to my ankles
Racing with you on the spaceship fuck
going warp 9
into other worlds
They say when we came
the moon moved

para Osita

Tenderly Your

hands open me into the drum of my heart
soft circle of your spirit where I'm always welcome
We're in the grass of prairies our grandmothers rode
Sweet smell of distant cookpots edges the blue
Your kisses are a hundred years old & newly born
rich as the red earth where you straddle a pinto
your fingers twined in leather
Ride me now as your hungry lips blow me softly
Flaming ride us past our rapes   our pain
past years when we stumbled lost
Yours are the hands I've dreamed
I hear your name in my pulse
This
is why we were made by creation
Wet song of our bellies
twining our fire

for Denise

Getting Down

to the bone place where blood is made
and every moon's a mother
your hands & tongue
in me a brush fire I wake up wanting you
Shrill cry of a dawn bird between my legs
memories of your sweet brown breasts
brushing my thighs
You go
where no one
has gone before until I'm weeping laughing
as you murmur in my wet ear
your husky voice like hot blood   *I love you*
My hair in your mouth burns for you
your lips nibble my lips my breasts
think they can't live without you
Between moments of you I'm a bird
who flies out of vision
You come
like the first bird breaking open the night with dawn
stars bursting into day sucking you I'm made
a moon sweet with light
Crying in the bone & blood place where you make me
yours

for Joanne

I Like a Woman Who Packs

not because she wants to be a man because she knows
I want a butch
who can loop my wrist with leather, whisper *Stay right here*
I have something I need to do to you
who can smile wide when I ask her to dance
because I've noticed the bulge in her pants
Tells me to come back for a slow number
because she doesn't do fast
I like a woman who'll make me beg her for it
Ride me till I forget my name, the date
the president, prime minister & every head of state
I like to sashay down the street a bit
with her watching my legs & breasts & ass
while I watch her hands & mouth
& the neighbors gasp
I like a woman who can make me over
into whatever she wants
as long as she wants
wet & hungry to my heart
I like it when she grabs my hair
says   *Don't move until I tell you*
I like a woman who packs
stands behind me in a crowded room leaning into my back
whispers in my ear
Hey you wanna give it up to me?
I like her tall or short   heavy or slim
walking or riding a chair   brown or pink   old or young
I like a woman who can take me under
when she takes me over

then let me suck her, get in trouble, snap her gloves
I like a woman who wants to be
the best fuck I've ever had
I like a woman who snacks

Up All Night Again

Red flower of your tongue
rests on my swollen
satisfied tenderness
as I drift a golden lake
flying wide
Sweet weight of your shoulders
on my thighs sings
in the rising sun

for Denise

Dream Lesbian Lover

is there when I get home from work but allows me silence
to unravel or better yet   isn't there
but has left a note & a little surprise
She rubs my feet for hours
She wants to love me till I can't stand no more
& she rolls over to me so sweet
Dream lover cooks me hot meals & washes up after
Never arrives without flowers & only brings my favorites
Dream lover has long fingers   a patient playful tongue
& thrives on 5 hours sleep a night
She could play the harmonica   weave pine needle baskets
bead me a wedding sash   write me lust poems
& love poems
Dream lover has eyes deep as the sky
feels herself in others
feels our connecting bones   Rises early in the morning
to make the best rich coffee
Aah   She could bring you to your knees with a look
& does
Dreamy woman has a bed of lace & roses & home
She could build a fire in the rain
Could always fix my car for free
Could call the dentist to make my appointment
Iron my shirt when I'm in a hurry
Knows how to make chocolate mousse   chocolate silk pie
black bottom cupcakes   molasses cookies
sour cream coffee cake   lemon pound cake
& fresh mango ice cream
O such a creamy dreamy one

She's showing up tonight with a butch pout
& a femme slink
a tough stance & a long knowing
Dream lover
she won't have any other girlfriends
but won't mind
if I do

A *Personals Ad*, with tongue in cheek

Two Butches

planned to take me out to dinner then surprise
me by taking me back to the toilet
one of them holding me down while the other
fucked my brains out
Boring I said   I did bathroom sex when I was too young
to know better & I'm a lot stronger than I look
I've got a better idea
Why don't you both
come home to my nice big 4-poster bed
of your own free will
I'll tie one of you to my easy
chair while the other one & I take our time
most of the night
After we've come that chair should be wet enough
I'll lick her pussy
until she's shouting to get out of those ropes
but she won't be able to do a damn
thing about it
except come

In the Wild River of Your Arms

where I'm carried to wet silk plunging
I lean into your strong back which doesn't give
in the sharp turns of touch
Bears me through nightmares & changing faces
lights racing a glitter of deep kisses
in darkness I didn't know was my home
until you held me & would not
let go

In the wild river of your laughter
nothing I do is crazy or too much
or can't be understood with time
No need for lies because you've no accusations
Grinning you embrace all that I am
even what I don't want of myself

In the wild river of your tongue
I travel light years away from everyone
who has lain with me claiming
some corner of my spirit as their own
read meanings into me
without my knowledge or consent
made me afraid of my own desire
ploughed me with confusion
as they called arid sand a verdant bank
tried to kill all
that surges clear in me
a wild river uncontained
without a name

In the wild river of your cunt
where I am first to shake you free & screaming wildly
I swim against the tide of brutal discarded husband
shame   & rocks of regret for a woman
who would not give you this water
we drink as though the desert burns on every side
I ride you lightly as a birch bark canoe
in late spring melt
catching your wrists in a seine of desire new
& trembling as this wind
breathing between us bringing song

In the wild river of your soul
I've known you clear green & true
your hands carry no deception no bribes
My brother calls you a good old gal
& loves your laugh
I remember the child I was before
my uncle sliced her into debris
I see a long ribbon of our lives
flashing with the hope of home
I thought couldn't be

In the wild river of your eyes
I wash up new alive with colors
I open the deep pool of my tenderness
& float you down
where our toes are dancing on rocks
like crawdads waving hello with long feelers

Light as a leaf boat skimming the lights
my tongue is fishing for your pleasure
sweet water sweet grass
in the wild river
of our arms

for Denise

Looking for a Blanket to Cover Myself
After the Horses Are Free

Journal Entry 7/9/93

I'm eating fresh island-grown organic raspberries, soft as clits, to celebrate my completion & delivery of the manuscript, even through the grief of Sapphocat's death   This is a foot-in-mouth book   My heart is angry that I feel compelled to justify my lust, that an explanation is necessary, that I already know I'll be misinterpreted when all I want & need to do is open my passion & let her gallop without reins   I'm very apprehensive about the response: I expect the rage of "vanilla" (how I dislike that term for its disrespect, & yet, have no other) as well as s/m Dykes   I'm hurt that so many of us have no appropriate boundaries, that we glamorize pain of all types into mystery or love, that I've only met 4 or 5 Lesbians who say they've never had sex with a man – either through rape or voluntarily   I'm tired of the dead roses of heterosexual romance & marriage which we ourselves slop over Lesbian sexuality and power   Exhausted with the denial about emotional abuse, which is rampant among us, especially the sort that rigidly condemns or mocks others without compassion

All of the s/m Dykes I'm close to (although this is not a generalization about s/m) are survivors of extreme abuse, some of which was life threatening (of which I am also a survivor)   The fact remains that men are still far more responsible, overwhelmingly so, for sexual violence against women, than women are   While I don't find whips erotic

& don't want to be whipped, I'm also clear that my real enemies are colonization, warfare, exploitation, racism & greed These tools & wreckages of the conquistador patriarch are enemies far more powerful than any s/m Dyke   As for violence in s/m, I know of a "nice," middle-class caucasian Lesbian who shot her lover (in the back) & killed her, & never went to jail because she had a "good" job, it was an "accident," a "crime of passion" (she was being left for another women) & she had a fancy lawyer   No Lesbian confronted her   Her act was swept under our very lumpy rug because it was too terrifying to absorb   We each mourned Karen silently, usually alone & often with booze

Where is our responsibility in this, as a gang struggling to become a community?   Why don't we say anything to the director of the (mostly heterosexual) battered women's shelter who batters her female partner?   And more troublesome still, *how* do we do this without ourselves becoming abusive?   As women, we have no models for non-violence (Ghandi had a sexual relationship with a minor)   We have no safe or sane place – only the illusion (easily shattered by a rapist) that we do   As I've been sexual with a number of Lesbians who define themselves as s/m, who were happy to have vanilla sex with me, & who were far more careful to ask what I wanted or didn't want than is usual (for many of us, sex is still "dirty" & is still expected to happen by some kind of nonverbal magic osmosis – a shard of heterosexuality, which has no need of communication because the norm is still male pleasure & female submission), I fail to under-

stand how the word *violence* is relevant   This does not
deny that s/m Lesbians have abused others, as all other
groups of people have   If a Lesbian can only reach orgasm
by being whipped, how can any of us claim the right to
deny her sexual pleasure?   I find this kind of denial partic-
ularly offensive, as I've been denounced on the congression-
al floor by jessie helms for my sexuality, & often find it
difficult to tell the difference between the arguments of the
extremist christians & Lesbians opposed to Lesbian Erotica
I claim this land   I celebrate our outlaw lust   There are no
weeds – only plants whose flowers or taste we dislike

Once, we were the Women's Liberation Movement   I'm
still fighting for Liberation, though not for feminism,
which has been gutted by academia   However much I
want no one ever to be whipped again, it is presumptuous
& oppressive to define another person's sexuality, when that
sexuality is consensual   Here we are in the very murky
waters of how a colonized people could claim that consen-
suality or freedom are even possible   I ask my friends not
to discuss certain of their practices with me, I've left situa-
tions I've found offensive, I tease & joke about what scares
me & I ignore publications that aren't erotic to me – return-
ing again & again to the actual enemies we face   These
enemies are so much more frightening than other Lesbians
– with all of our differences – which is why we attack those
whom we need as comrades (as Franz Fanon commented so
long ago), when we disagree with what they eat or do in
bed   So I can only say to critics: you have no right to

judge my sexuality or my experience   You can say this is poorly written or not erotic to you or boring or frightening   I, in turn, have the right not to participate in s/m *and* to be as supportive to those who do as it is possible for me to be   We long for black & white so we don't have to think or understand, but sex is every color of the rainbow & hanky code   We're still shouting at one another instead of listening

The Night Gown

In the troubled waters of Lesbian sexuality, where many of us are lying to each other & living inside media/society lies about us, I've tried to be as honest & inclusive in this collection as possible   As sex is both sacred & profane, funny as well as gross, tender & fierce, this erotica contains many voices, romantic as well as raunchy, some of which have since been discarded   My hope is that it will stay in bedrooms, well-thumbed, spilled on, bent back & squashed, a book that no one returns

Because sex has been split off from us as women in a colonizer culture, we ourselves police our pleasure   We consistently confuse the need for affection with sex, refuse to acknowledge the very real differences among us in terms of frequency of desire, often wallow for years not knowing what really excites us or how to ask another Lesbian to help us find out   We need to engage in a radical discussion & redefinition of our sexuality, a discussion which has been co-opted to issues of biology (abortion & conception), rather than sexual freedom, remembering that freedom needs the bones of responsibility to flourish

I've observed that ethics are not common or valued, & the lack of ethics contributes greatly to the pain of being a Lesbian   I believe this is internalized homophobia: we're "outlaws," so therefore we don't *need* ethics   No one respects us, so why should we respect each other?   I'm non-monogamous, and I've found that developing a code of personal ethics is essential to enjoyment of desire   I want to establish

the matrix of my sexuality & this writing in an ethical con-
text: I don't have sex with lovers of friends (or ex-lovers of
ex-lovers, etc.) nor with anyone under 18 or whose circum-
stances are so different from mine that I could be seen to
have power over them (e.g., a student of mine); I never have
sex with someone who defines herself as being in a monog-
amous relationship with someone else; I don't lie about one
lover to another   All of these rules have emerged from the
painful grit of experience   I'm as jealous as anyone, per-
haps more so, but I treat it as a symptom of my insecurity,
not as a right or an excuse to abuse a lover   I cope with it
myself or with a friend   I want neither to be owned nor to
own anyone   Perhaps my early experiences have affected
my trust of the ideal of fidelity, but I also have been told in
confidence of too many secret Lesbian affairs to think that
monogamy is practiced as often as it's preached   I prefer
reality to lies

This is my personal experience, with some exaggerations for
lace, not a bible with which to thump anyone over the head
Because it contains material which can easily be misunder-
stood, I will define my terms as clearly as possible

I've read all of the marquis de sade & henry miller, because
it is crucial to understand the mind of one's enemies   They
jointly define women as receptacles for whatever men desire
I define s/m rather strictly (yes, I intend the word play), as
de sade would, to describe pain and/or humiliation of one's
sexual partner   It is important to note that his victims were

not engaged in consensual sex & that he murdered an unknown number of servant-class women before he transgressed boundaries & killed a woman of a more privileged class, for which he was imprisoned the remainder of his life   His work was written in prison (a posh one, because he was of the ruling class), thus it has a very masturbatory flavor & it is difficult to know if he is describing actual acts or fantasies   His peers considered him a monster – not because he killed "under-class" women, or because of his sexual appetites, which many of them shared, but because he didn't hide his behavior   It has also been suggested that he was a madman that the catholic church scapegoated in order to hide the atrocities of the monks, who were at the time consolidating their political power   This is the man for whom sadism is named, perhaps inaccurately

Lesbianism is based in a belief that between women, power is shared, which makes it a radical act   This consensuality & this reverence for pleasure over procreation offends societies & threatens churches which operate in hierarchies of dominance & control   For those of us who cherish the concept of equality between women, it is extremely difficult to acknowledge the unseen & unspoken dominance & control of Lesbian life   I attempt to address this issue in the piece "Top Sadist in Town"

If one spends an hour sober in any Dyke bar (that isn't predominantly Lesbians of Color, & few are), you'll observe every aspect of heterosexually defined attractiveness, including the concept that the "hottest" Lesbian is young, slim, able-bodied & often blonde   She is not fat or old or quietly contemplating the scene   As we've internalized all these criteria for attractiveness, we have also absorbed the erotic charge of dominance and power

Much in our lives is dishonest   Lying is a necessary cornerstone of colonizer society, therefore lying about our sexuality feels "natural"   Thus, betrayal of trust is the most common theme of Lesbian gossip and dialogue   As long as we lie to each other, we have no relationship

It is risky & unsafe for me to be this open   Many of the behaviors I describe (fantasy play, use of dildoes, enjoyment of leather, bondage) are commonly considered s/m, although I disagree & consider my historically based definition of s/m more accurate, particularly because those behaviors were often a part of Lesbianism when I came out in the sixties (prior to the public s/m groups)

Many women use dildoes & simply don't say so, or carve squashes to avoid the embarrassment of a sex store   Many women tie one another up or spank one another but are afraid to say so because of the censorship of sexuality that has occurred since academic feminism invaded Lesbianism It is my belief that the rise of so-called s/m (which is often not behavior based in pain or humiliation, but where else can a Dyke with a dildo go?) is a defensive response to the feminist nonsense that arrogantly proposed feminism as the

theory & Lesbianism as the practice   Lesbianism is not
the possession of feminism   I'm not an academic, but I un-
derstand that this suppression is deliberate & sex-phobic
Middle-class addiction to niceness has created a split that I
feel is unnecessary   The christian right which wants to kill
queers doesn't care if you only have sex the nice girl way

Compassion & respect are virtues each of us needs to culti-
vate passionately   As one example of how dangerous it is
to pass judgment, I'll comment on something I've done re-
cently which illustrates how uneasily sexual definitions hold
For a good 2 months in the beginning of a relationship, I
badgered a woman to let me eat her pussy (a vanilla act I
adore), which she refused because she hates oral sex   Often
I can be very dense & selfish   It finally occurred to me that
this was abusive (under the guise of humor & teasing) & I
stopped   This is an instance of vanilla sex being used as a
means of dominance & control

Because homophobia is still a part of my community as a
First Nations woman, it is very difficult for me to publish
this book   I've decided to weather all possible storms in or-
der to make the book I needed to find in a bookstore when
I was 17   All of the women to whom various pieces have
been dedicated have given me their permission   For me
the difference between exploitive pornography and celebra-
tion of our glorious sexuality is rooted in ethical decisions &
mutual consent

Over the years, I've sadly watched women-only spaces de-crease until I only know of 2 or 3 worldwide   Our freedom to speak to each other has been co-opted   We have no control over who reads our work, but I want to be clear that this work is a gift given to other Lesbians   I don't want to be used by those who do not share my oppression or who are not working to end it

Now that I've covered my ass, sealed my reputation as a troublemaker & raised some eyebrows (& hopefully some more interesting body parts), I'll wish you, my Dyke friends, a very wet night, with as much satisfaction as you can conjure

Thanks & Bouquets

to all of my lovers, who continue to delight & inspire me
(no, you can't have their #s)

to the s/m community, which has been open to me despite
my opinions and especially helpful in clarifying my sexual
desire & limits   Their contribution to the visibility of Lesbian
sexuality is a valuable one

to the Lannan Foundation, whose financial support
made some of this work possible

to Gloria Jennifer Jackson Yamato, deer friend,
whose exploration of erotica has profoundly informed my own

to Karen Fredrickson,
for the idea of returning to the phrase Women's Liberation

to my many patient friends,
who often don't hear from me for months

to Hopscotch House & the artists there, where I was
so beautifully cared for as a writer

and especially
to the over 100 First Nations Lesbians I've met
in Canada, the United States, Mexico & New Zealand
whose beauty & courage help make my life possible

CHRYSTOS was born November 7, 1946, off reservation, to a Menominee father and a Lithuanian/Alsace-Lorraine mother. Raised in San Francisco and now living in the Pacific Northwest, she is a self-educated artist and writer, and an activist for numerous Native Rights & Prisoners' causes. She is the author of *Not Vanishing* (1988) and *Dream On* (1991). Her writing has been widely anthologized, including in *This Bridge Called My Back; A Gathering of Spirit; Gay & Lesbian Poetry of Our Time; Intricate Passions; Making Face, Making Soul/Haciendo Caras; Living the Spirit; InVersions: Writing by Dykes, Queers and Lesbians;* and *Piece of My Heart.*

In 1990 she received a National Endowment for the Arts grant for literature and in 1991 she was awarded a Lannan Foundation fellowship for poetry. She travels extensively throughout North America for readings and speaking engagements.

PRESS GANG PUBLISHERS FEMINIST CO-OPERATIVE
is committed to producing quality books with social and literary
merit. We prioritize Canadian women's work and include writing
by lesbians and by women from diverse cultural and class
backgrounds. Our list features vital and provocative
fiction, poetry and non-fiction.

A free catalogue is available from Press Gang Publishers
101 - 225 East 17th Ave., Vancouver, B.C. v5v 1A6 Canada